CREATIVE RESIN

EASY TECHNIQUES FOR CONTEMPORARY RESIN ART

Mia Winston-Hart

DAVID & CHARLES

www.davidandcharles.com

CONTENTS

INTRODUCTION 6

SAFETY 8

TOOLS & MATERIALS 10

TYPES OF RESIN 12

MOULDS FOR RESIN CASTING 14

RESIN CRAFTING TOOLS 17

COLOUR 18

INSERTIONS 20

JEWELLERY ESSENTIALS 22

TECHNIQUES 24

HOW TO MIX AND POUR 26

HOW TO AVOID BUBBLES 29

HOW TO LAYER 30

HOW TO DE-MOULD 31

HOW TO DRY FLOWERS 32

HOW TO MAKE A CUSTOM MOULD 34

PROJECTS 36

PEARL-DROP FLOWER EARRINGS 38

INTO THE FOREST PENDANT 42

FORGET-ME-NOT NECKLACE 46

ENGRAVED FAN EARRINGS 50

SHIMMERING ABSTRACT COASTER 56

FAUX MARBLE COASTERS 60

ANIMAL PRINT MAKE-UP TRAY 64

OCEAN WAVES SERVING TRAY 68

GALAXY SIDE TABLE 74

MOTHER-OF-PEARL MERMAID'S COMB 80

GOLDEN FLORAL KEY RING 84

KEEPSAKE PHOTO KEY RING 88

SUPER SPARKLY HAIR CLIP 92

SHAKE IT UP HAIR CLIP 96

MAPLE LEAF PHONE CASE 102

POSY PAPERWEIGHT 106

CORAL HOOP EARRINGS 110

TROUBLESHOOTING 116

ABOUT THE AUTHOR 118

ACKNOWLEDGMENTS 118

SUPPLIERS 118

INDEX 119

CREATIVE RESIN

EASY TECHNIQUES FOR CONTEMPORARY RESIN ART

Mia Winston-Hart

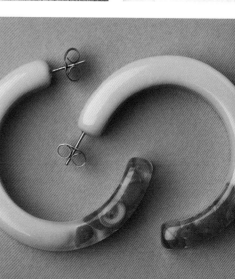

INTRODUCTION

Resin can be manipulated into any shape you desire and can be coloured in many beautiful ways. It allows you to capture botanical elements at their very best forever, or to commemorate special moments by perfectly preserving sentimental objects. Once used almost exclusively industrially, its rise in popularity over the last few years has seen the development of many types of resin tailored specifically for the crafting market. Working with resin will require some patience, yet it is extremely therapeutic and I am delighted to be able to introduce you to its creative possibilities.

Once I had discovered resin, I quickly became obsessed with the myriad ways in which it can be used. There is such a fantastic range of supplies on the market now to support this up-and-coming craft, from moulds of any shape you can imagine, to pigments and glitters in all the colours of the rainbow, and so much more. There are so many ways in which you can manipulate resin to create beautiful accessories, including jewellery, keepsakes, homewares and more besides.

In this book I will teach you all about the different kinds of resin available and what they're used for. We'll explore the wonderful world of moulds, discover ways to colour resin, and identify insertions that can make your creations really special. You'll learn how to mix and pour resin to achieve the very best results, and how to avoid unsightly bubbles or de-moulding disasters. There are useful extras too, including how to dry flowers, how to finish jewellery to a professional standard, and how to make a custom-made mould to enable you to turn the ideas you dream about into tangible pieces.

It is my hope that the techniques you learn in this book will encourage you to take things even further, especially when it comes to mould making! Whether you're learning how to use resin as a hobby or as a business, it is important to remember to trust and enjoy the process. Be sure to treat the resin with respect – you are working with chemicals after all – but, although you obviously need to be careful, it is still possible to have lots of fun and to enjoy every moment of this creative hobby.

SAFETY

Resins produced for the craft market are perfectly safe to use as long as you follow the health and safety recommendations of the manufacturer. Remember, resin is a chemical so always work carefully.

For the projects featured in this book, I have used resins from Resin8 (see Suppliers), following their recommendations in regards to PPE (personal protection equipment). PPE requirements will vary depending on the type of resin being used, as each has different chemical qualities that need to be taken into account, but the list that follows sets out the very minimum safety practices that you should observe:

· Always work in a well-ventilated room.

· Wear nitrile gloves (or use a specialist resin barrier cream on your hands); be aware that the chemicals in resin can break down other plastics, so don't be tempted to use standard household gloves.

· Always wear a respirator when sanding resin.

· Always wear safety goggles when working with large volumes of resin or when sanding.

· Avoid skin contact - always wear a long-sleeved top to protect your arms and a full-length apron to protect your clothes; accidental resin spills cannot be washed off, so old clothes are best!

· Don't eat, drink or smoke while working with resin.

· If you get anything in your eye, wash with plenty of water for 15 minutes and seek medical advice immediately.

PROTECTING YOUR WORK SURFACE

I have a messy studio, so I don't mind if the surfaces I am working on get resin on them, but if you don't want this to happen to your table at home, protect it with a silicone mat; bin bags taped down with masking tape make a good alternative. Keep a pot of baby wipes close to hand to clear up any small spills or to wipe your gloves clean if they get too sticky.

DEALING WITH AN EXOTHERMIC REACTION

If you carefully read and observe the instructions provided by the manufacturer of your chosen resin products, this is extremely unlikely to happen, but it's best to be prepared. When resin cures, it lets off a small amount of heat - and if this happens too quickly (if you are mixing too large a batch, for example) an exothermic reaction may occur. The resin will begin to smoke and may catch fire. If you do find yourself in a situation where this is happening, move your pot of resin to somewhere safe; outside your home is best. Once you have done so, watch the resin from a distance, wait for the reaction to finish and for the resin to cool, then bin it.

Always read the data sheets that come with your resin for specific PPE requirements and consult your resin supplier for further advice if necessary.

It is imperative when sanding resin to wear a mask: Resin8 recommend the 3M 4251 Organic Vapour and Particulate Respirator.

TOOLS & MATERIALS

TYPES OF RESIN

There are three main types of resin – epoxy, UV and polyester. Polyester resin is an industrial resin that cures extremely quickly, leaving a strong smell for days after use, and it is not suitable for crafting. I most often use epoxy resin in my work, and sometimes UV resin, so let's take a look at these in a little more detail.

EPOXY RESIN

Epoxy resin is my preferred choice for making jewellery as well as other small to medium items. There are many different brands available, but for the projects in this book I have used those from Resin8 (see Suppliers). Each resin manufacturer has its own product names for their epoxy resins, but in essence there are two different types: shallow pour and deep pour. Your choice will be determined by the size of the object to be made.

Epoxy resins come in two parts, one part being the resin and the other the hardener – Resin8 refers to these as part A (resin) and part B (hardener). When these two parts are mixed, a chemical reaction takes place that, over a period of time, hardens the material to a solid plastic (a process referred to as curing). Each product has a different mixing ratio and although most commonly this is either 1:1 (one part resin and one part hardener) or 2:1 (two parts resin and one part hardener), other more specific mixing ratios may be required. It is very important, therefore, to make sure you read the instructions that come with your purchased resin carefully and to always mix to the recommended ratios. You should never mix different brands of resin together or resins with different mixing ratios.

SHALLOW POUR RESIN

Shallow pour resins can only be poured into a mould no deeper than 1cm (⅜in) in depth. Pour deeper than this and the risk of an exothermic reaction increases. When resin cures, it lets off a small amount of heat, and when a deep amount of a shallow pour resin is poured, it can heat up very quickly. If this happens it will let off enough heat to smoke, releasing toxic fumes, and it may potentially catch fire. However, this is very unlikely to happen, especially if you carefully observe the instructions provided by the manufacturer. If a large amount of shallow pour resin is required for larger moulds, it is recommended that the resin be mixed in several smaller batches to minimize the heat generated. Stick to the rules and all should be fine.

I have used Coat-it resin from Resin8 for the majority of the projects in this book. This is a 1:1 mix (one part A to one part B) for shallow pours. Depending on room conditions, it should be touch dry within 24 hours and fully cured after 21 days.

For what to do in the event of an exothermic reaction, see Safety.

DEEP POUR RESIN

Resins that are suitable for a deeper pour typically take a lot longer to cure than shallow pour resins. Widely used for table art, memorial pieces and for working with deep moulds, these are often mixed in a 2:1 ratio (two parts resin to one part hardener). The mixed resin is usually very runny, which means that there are likely to be fewer bubbles. Crystal clear and easy to work with, this type of resin will just take a long time to cure!

I have used Fill-it from Resin8 for the Posy Paperweight project. This is a 2:1 mix used for deep pours that can be safely poured to a depth of 5cm (2in) in one layer. Depending on room conditions, it should be touch dry within 3-4 days and fully cured after 21 days.

Drying and curing times can vary drastically from one resin manufacturer to another, so always read the information on the bottle as well as the product sheet provided.

HEATPROOF RESIN

Heatproof epoxy resins are also available and these are brilliant for making items such as coasters. The mixing ratio for these resins will vary depending on the brand, although 1:1 or 2:1 are most common. Sometimes heatproof epoxy resin can be more expensive, so it is often more economical to use it as a coating layer only. For example, you could use a shallow pour resin in the coaster mould; then, once it has cured and been de-moulded, apply a top coat of heat-resistant resin onto the surface that the cup would sit on.

It is important to note that the heat resistance of the resin needs to develop over a period of time. You will find that, even though the resin has cured, the length of time recommended by the manufacturer before use is so much longer. Most require 28 days, although the developing time will vary across different brands, so always check the instructions carefully.

A word of warning: Never use heatproof resin for any item that holds an open flame, such as candles or ash trays, as this poses a serious fire risk. If you are making tea light holders, battery-operated tealights that mimic a flickering flame will look just as beautiful!

UV RESIN

UV resin can be used for jewellery pieces, although this is not something I would recommend: it is fragile and items made from nothing but this resin can break easily if dropped. However, I do like to use it for those occasions when waiting for epoxy resin to cure isn't a suitable option, such as sealing filled cavities on shaker moulds (see the Shake It Up Hair Clip project). UV resin comes in pre-mixed bottles so it can be squeezed out exactly where it is needed, and it cures in around 3 minutes under a UV light.

MOULDS FOR RESIN CASTING

Once mixed, resin is poured into a mould to cast it into a shape to make any number of different items. In this book I have mainly chosen to work with moulds for smaller pieces such as jewellery, key rings and hair clips, and a small selection of the exciting range of moulds available on the market is pictured here.

BUYING MOULDS

When purchasing a mould for resin casting, I would always recommend choosing a silicone mould, especially when casting jewellery pieces using epoxy resin. Silicone moulds are very flexible, making de-moulding easier, and they result in beautifully shiny pieces if you are using a shiny mould!

It's worth remembering that if you want a shiny finish to your cast resin piece, then you need a shiny mould. If, however, you would like a frosted or a matt finish, then your mould also needs to be frosted or matt.

As well as single piece moulds, look out for multiple piece jewellery moulds, as these enable you to produce many component pieces at once. They are often themed according to the type of item to be made, for example earring or hair clip shapes; or sometimes by motif, such as hearts, flowers or geometric shapes.

Some moulds for pendants, earrings and key rings have been designed to cast pieces with a ready-made hole, so that you can add a jump ring, fit an earring hoop or attach a key ring chain without having to drill a hole for finishing. I prefer to use moulds that create solid pieces as it gives me more options of how to use them, but if not having to drill holes appeals to you, look out for 'no-drill' moulds.

Shaker moulds enable you to include free-floating insertions in your resin, as they have raised areas for filling with a suitable liquid, such as baby oil. They come in all sorts of fun designs and I have used a shaker mould to make the Shake It Up Hair Clip.

The majority of the projects in this book use shallow pour resins for small items, but for the Posy Paperweight I have ventured into the world of deep pour resins, working with a 3D domed mould. There are many suitable moulds available if you want to explore this technique further.

Colourful silicone moulds can really brighten up your work space, but it is important to remember that while you can use moulds of any colour when working with epoxy resin, if you do choose to cast with UV resin you must use a clear mould to ensure that the UV light can access the resin fully, otherwise your piece won't cure.

For step-by-step instruction on how to make a custom mould for jewellery making, see Techniques: How to make a custom mould.

USING OBJECTS AS MOULDS

A few of the projects featured use everyday objects to cast creative resin pieces, such as a lipped edge metal table (see Galaxy Side Table) and a mobile phone shell (see Maple Leaf Phone Case). I hope that projects such as these will encourage you to explore and to discover what items you can transform with resin in your own home.

USING INSERTIONS IN MOULDS

If you are using insertions in your resin (see Tools & Materials: Inserts), you should always check which will be the top side of the finished piece once it is de-moulded and place your items accordingly.

If the mould has a shiny inner, the chances are that this will become the top of the piece once it is de-moulded, as the shiny side will give a super-smooth texture. So, in this instance, items such as pressed or dried flowers or photographs should be placed in the mould right side facing down.

CARING FOR YOUR MOULDS

Over time, the chemical reaction that takes place as the resin cures will affect your moulds and they will deteriorate. With careful use, you should be able to pour in the same mould up to 15 times; however, applying heat to your moulds will make them deteriorate faster. To extend the life of your moulds, I recommend the bubble fishing method rather than the heating method for removing bubbles from resin (see Techniques: How to avoid bubbles).

To keep your moulds in prime condition, keep them in a box separate to your other supplies. Make sure to stack them neatly in the box and avoid folding or bending them.

To clean your moulds, use baby wipes to remove any sticky remnants. If you are left with small, dry pieces of resin in the mould, use a little tape to pull them off – this works amazingly well for stuck bits of glitter, too. Never be tempted to clean moulds by rinsing them in the sink: resin is harmful to aquatic life when uncured, and after curing it is considered a micro-plastic.

When your moulds have started to stick to your resin, or become dull when they were once shiny, or are damaged in any way, they're not fixable and it's time to buy new ones!

RESIN CRAFTING TOOLS

In addition to the all-important resin and the moulds you choose to use, there are a few everyday essentials that you will need for crafting with resin. The good news is that you are likely to have most of these in your home already!

DIGITAL SCALES
Digital scales are essential to accurately measure the two components required to mix the epoxy resin. Remember to select the millilitre option.

SILICONE MATS
A large silicone mat will help to keep your surface clean and protected while you work – things can get messy! A small silicone mat will be useful, too, for more delicate jobs, such as coating small pressed flowers with resin.

PLASTIC CUPS
I generally use disposable plastic cups for mixing my resin in. Silicone mixing cups in various sizes are also available, which can be cleaned and reused, although not without some considerable effort!

MIXING STICKS
Although silicone mixing sticks are available, I find that wooden lolly sticks work just fine; I also use them for coating as well as mixing.

TOOTHPICKS
These are mainly used to carefully add pigments to your resin, as often only a very small amount is required. They are also useful for teasing resin into thin or narrow areas of a mould.

BABY WIPES
You are going to need lots of these, for cleaning sticky moulds, sticky (gloved) hands, sticky work surfaces, and mopping up any resin spills.

STICKY TAPE
This is useful to pull off any small pieces of cured resin that have stuck to your moulds.

HEAT GUN
I use a heat gun to create exciting surface effects such as those on the Ocean Waves Serving Tray. Caution should always be taken when using any hot tool; follow all health and safety guidelines provided by the heat gun supplier as well as specific advice on heating resin as supplied by the resin manufacturer.

REJUVEN8 POLISHING COLLECTION
I have used this to achieve the super-shiny finish on the Coral Hoop Earrings project, which provides a masterclass on how to use the collections! It includes six different grades of wet-and-dry sandpaper (180, 240, 400, 800, 1200, 2500 grits), two cloths, one abrasive paste (scratch remover) and one gloss spray (shine enhancer). The sandpapers should be used wet to minimize dust, but even so you must always wear a mask with organic vapour filters when sanding resin.

For PPE recommendations, including advice on gloves, googles and masks, see Safety.

COLOUR

There are various ways to colour your resin and the effects achieved will vary depending on what you choose. The colouring medium I favour is opaque pigment, which I've used for almost all the projects in this book. I love how, with just a basic primary colour palette plus black and white, you can make any colour you wish. But let's explore your other options, too.

PIGMENTS

Resin pigments are available in either opaque (rich and dense) or transparent (vivid and translucent) colours. They have the texture of a sticky paste and can be added in small amounts to mixed resin. You can choose from a wide range of ready-made colours or mix your own colour prior to adding it to the resin.

Always add just a small amount of colour at a time and always follow the manufacturer's instructions to the letter; if you add too much, your resin may not cure properly.

Mixed resins that have had different colours added to them can be simultaneously poured into the same mould to give interesting effects as they run together, as can be seen in the Mother-of-Pearl Mermaid's Comb project.

MICAS

Made from natural minerals, mica powder when added to your resin in small quantities can give it a shimmery look. It comes in a variety of colours, of course, so there are plenty of opportunities to explore the results that can be achieved. When making moulds I always add mica to my silicone as I love the pop of colour that it provides (see Techniques: How to make a custom mould), but I can think of lots of ways in which you can get creative with it. Here are just a few:

- Add just a small amount of mica to any opaque coloured resin to give it a subtle shimmer.
- Pour two mixed resins, each coloured with a different mica powder, into the same mould and watch the effect as they blend together.
- Add mica powder to an opaque white resin for a pearly, cloud-like effect.

ALCOHOL INKS

Densely coloured and alcohol based, these inks can be added to your clear resin in two ways. You can add a small amount into the resin as it is mixed to create a transparently coloured resin. Alternatively, you can pour your mixed resin into the mould, then add the ink drop by drop (photo 1). The petri-dish effect is a good way to explore this method. Drop a few drops of white ink onto the colour ink (photo 2), then add another colour and again apply a few more drops of white ink (photo 3). Once de-moulded, the finished results can be quite dramatic.

A word of warning: Never use any form of open flame near or on alcohol inks.

Don't be tempted to use acrylic paint or water-based colouring media to colour your resin. It can cause an exothermic reaction in your resin or prevent it from setting properly.

Once the shape is de-moulded, the full glory of the petri-dish effect is revealed. The white ink has the highest density, so it has sunk towards the bottom of the mould (now the front!), creating abstract areas of colour.

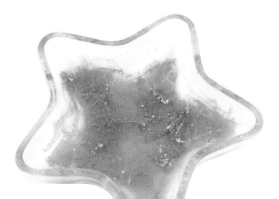

1

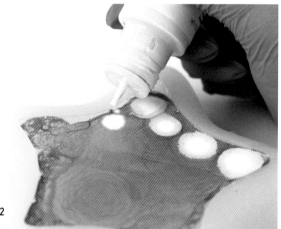

2

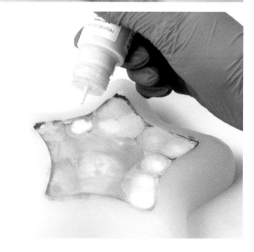

3

INSERTIONS

There are many pretty things you can add to your resin, including flowers, foils and glitters. There are a few key things to remember when working with insertions such as these, which I have outlined below.

FLOWERS

When working with flowers, they need to be completely dry (see Techniques: How to dry flowers). Dried flowers are very lightweight and will float in your resin, which is why I generally prefer to use them in layered resin work, to ensure that they are encapsulated perfectly to protect their delicate form.

If you are using a small mould, use a small flower. Small flowers that work well and retain their colour and shape include daisies, pansies, violas and forget-me-nots. These are all excellent for making jewellery as they fit well into the small moulds. Pressed flowers work best for small moulds and shallow pours.

When working with deep pour resin, bigger dried flowers come into their own as you can fit them nicely into the larger moulds without worrying about space. Choose robust flowers, such as roses, chrysanthemums and large daisies; other delicate flowers like peonies do work well, too, but you will need to be very patient and careful.

FOILS

Gold, silver and copper foil are very popular and easy to source but you can find other colours too. Foils are quite lightweight and have a tendency to float, so working in layers may be best depending on the project you are making. There are a few tips I can share with you to get the best results when adding foils to your resin:

- Work away from a draught to avoid the foil pieces being blown everywhere.
- Make sure to wipe your gloved hands clean to remove any stickiness, otherwise you will end up with more foil on your gloves than in your mould.
- Take your time and work slowly for best results.
- As an alternative to adding the foil to your resin, brush the foil into the mould before pouring the resin in, as I did with the Animal Print Make-up Tray.

GLITTER

There is so much choice when it comes to glitter in terms of both colour and texture. Some are ultrafine, some are chunky, and then there are the texture/colour mixes! You can buy themed shapes too, which are great at Christmas and Halloween.

Glitter can be tricky to work with, as you may have the opposite problem to floating flowers and foils. Often glitter is heavier than the resin and it can therefore sink to the bottom to form its own layer; this is especially true of chunky glitter. There are a couple of things you can do to prevent this. One option is to add the glitter to your resin once it has thickened slightly. Another option is to combine glitter and mixed resin with a 1:1 mixing ratio, so that when you pour the resin it will be heavily saturated with glitter and no separation line will be visible. Note that fine glitters will suspend in resin better than chunky ones.

I have seen artists encapsulate many things in resin, including dried insects, biscuits and locks of hair! So, as long as whatever you intend to use is completely dry, you can be as adventurous as you wish.

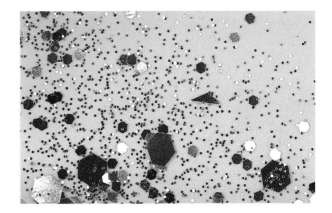

JEWELLERY ESSENTIALS

I am probably best known for my jewellery resin designs, and it is this that has been the inspiration for many of the projects in this book. Here I'll walk you through my jewellery-making essentials, the tools and findings I use on a daily basis to help me to achieve professional pieces quickly and easily.

JEWELLERY-MAKING TOOLS

There are just a couple of essential tools required to turn your resin pieces into wearable jewellery:

· **Rotary tool or small hand drill with various sizes of drill bits:** For drilling holes in finished resin pieces to attach jump rings to, which can then be attached to earring hoops or necklace (or key ring) chains. These are easy to source online and an angler's tackle drill is an inexpensive option if you are just starting out; but if you are drilling lots of pieces a day, you would be wise to invest in a heavy-duty option, as it will be stronger and therefore quicker to work with.

· **Two small pairs of jewellery pliers:** For attaching jump rings or other findings through drilled holes. Jewellery pliers are small and easy to hold and two pairs are required to work quickly and efficiently. Flat-nosed jewellery pliers with rubber-tipped jaws are best as they won't chip the enamel on coloured jump rings.

DRILLING A HOLE

The first thing to consider is the size of your jump ring to the size of your drill bit: for the jump ring to move freely, I recommend sizing up by 0.5mm when selecting your drill bit – so, for example, for a jump ring made from 1mm thick metal wire, use a 1.5mm drill bit.

When using the drill, work on a supported surface that you do not mind damaging. I normally work by eye, as I have had a lot of practice, but if you prefer you can use a pen to mark the exact position of the hole before starting to drill.

Drill slowly and firmly: if you work too fast, you may slip and make a mistake.

JEWELLERY FINDINGS

Findings are pieces that link elements together in the process of making jewellery and a selection of these are pictured here. For making the pieces in this book you will need jump rings, ball pins, earring hooks, hoops and studs. Silver- or gold-plated, sterling silver or stainless steel, the choice is yours.

ATTACHING A JUMP RING

One of the key tasks in making jewellery is fitting a jump ring, either to a jewellery finding or to a cast resin piece. If done incorrectly you can bend the delicate metal in the process, so be sure to follow this simple step-by-step for perfect results every time. Remember, always work with two pairs of jewellery pliers.

1   To open the jump ring, grip it between two pairs of pliers on either side of the join and as close to the join as possible.

2   Twist one hand towards you and the other hand away from you to open the join just enough to be able to fit through the piece you are connecting to the jump ring.

3   Once you have threaded on your resin piece or finding, grip on either side of the join as before and twist to close, so that the ends of the join neatly meet.

There are so many additions to explore when making jewellery, including brass charms, tassels, semi-precious beads and lots more!

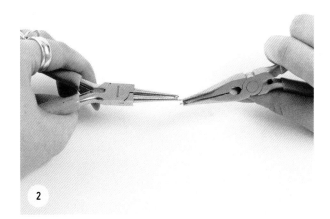

TECHNIQUES

HOW TO MIX AND POUR

This is the most important part of working with resin; if you go wrong here, you will find that you can't fix your mistake further down the line. It will determine how successful your finished piece will be. Resin that is not mixed correctly will not set and can remain bendy, and resin that is not poured correctly may end up full of unsightly bubbles.

MEASURING AND MIXING

Resins can be mixed in different ratios depending on the brand, type of resin and what it is to be used for. Most resins will be a 1:1 or a 2:1 mix ratio (see Tools & Materials: Types of resin for further information). Always follow the instructions provided by the manufacturer. Remember, never mix different resin brands or resins with different mix ratios together.

The resin instructions will provide the mix ratio, but how do you determine how much resin to mix overall? Many mould manufacturers give advice on the amount of resin required to fill their moulds, but if this is not provided or you are working without a mould, there is an easy way to check how much you will need. Fill your mould with water to the required depth (if you are working in layers, for example, you may only need to half fill), then pour out the water into a cup and measure it to give you your answer (see How to measure, step 1, for using digital scales to measure liquids). Do make sure that you wipe your mould with a dry cloth afterwards so that no water remains.

MEASURING AND MIXING LARGE BATCHES OF RESIN

As mentioned in Tools & Materials: Types of resin, certain resins can only be poured to certain depths and the same applies for mixing too. When working with shallow pour resins you need to be careful not to mix large batches of resin all in the same cup, as this may cause an exothermic reaction (where resin can smoke and release toxic fumes). It is advisable, therefore, for larger projects that require a lot of shallow pour resin, such as the Animal Print Make-up Tray and the Galaxy Side Table, to mix the resin in multiple cups.

Deep pour resins are designed to be used with deeper moulds, so it is safer to mix it in fewer cups than it would be for a shallow pour resin.

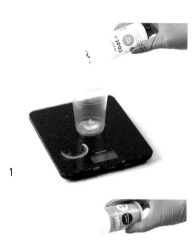

1

2

3

HOW TO MEASURE

Once you have determined how much resin you need to mix and therefore how much of part A (resin) to part B (hardener), it's time to get measuring. I recommend investing in a set of digital scales with a millimetre setting option for absolute accuracy.

1 Place the empty mixing cup on the scales and only then press the on button. This will ensure that you do not accidentally weigh the cup! Check that you have selected the millimetre setting. Pour in part A until you have measured the amount required.

2 Leaving the mixing cup on the scales, pour in part B, working to the mix ratio required. Work slowly to avoid adding too much.

3 As you reach the necessary total, you can use a mixing stick to add small amounts so that you do not pour in too much.

Mixing slowly and carefully will help prevent bubbles; you can read more about this in How to avoid bubbles.

HOW TO MIX

When you have poured your resin (part A first, then part B) into a mixing cup, you need to mix it carefully so that it is suitable to work with. The resin manufacturer will recommend a mixing time, but this is not likely to be less than 3 minutes. The three key things to remember are:

· Make sure that you mix in one direction only. I work in a clockwise direction.

· Do not lift the mixing stick up and out of the resin and then back into the resin as this will add air bubbles to your mixture, which is something you want to avoid.

· Make sure that you are scraping the sides and bottom of the cup as you mix so that the two parts are fully mixed; this ensures that you will achieve the correct mix ratio so that the resin cures properly.

DE-BUBBLING

Once your resin has been mixed, I recommend leaving it to sit and 'de-bubble' for about 10 minutes before pouring. This allows the bubbles to come to the surface of the resin and burst; if they don't burst of their own accord, you can remove them with a mixing stick and place them into a spare cup to be disposed of.

De-bubbling is particularly important for projects that have botanical inclusions. The tiny mushrooms in the Into the Forest Pendant, for example, can hold little bubbles within their crevices.

POURING

When you pour your (hopefully) bubble-free resin into the mould, remember that it is easier to add more resin than it is to take it away.

1   Pour slowly as you fill your mould, as this will help to avoid introducing bubbles during the pouring stage.

2   If you are working with a small mould, you can use your mixing stick to drop tiny amounts of resin into it to avoid overfilling.

3   A correctly filled mould should look like the one in this photograph.

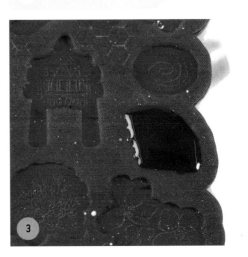

HOW TO AVOID BUBBLES

Bubbly resin is something that you want to avoid at all costs: it can create holes in your finished piece as well as sharp corners, and it can make the resin appear blurry rather than clear. So let's look at some ways to avoid those pesky bubbles.

RESIN TEMPERATURE

Epoxy resin is susceptible to temperature conditions and if it gets too cold you may notice that part A (resin) looks as if it has crystallized. If this happens, fill a jug with hot water and leave the resin bottle in the water until the particles dissolve (photo 1). This makes the consistency thinner, which is also likely to result in fewer bubbles when working with the resin.

MIXING

When mixing up your resin, remember to always mix slowly and in the same direction, keeping the mixing stick low in the cup. You should not be pulling the resin up out of the cup with your mixing stick as this will create lots of bubbles!

Remember to leave the resin to de-bubble for a short time to let the bubbles rise and disperse (photo 2). You can use your mixing stick to hook out any bubbles that remain (photo 3).

POURING

Pour slowly, a little at a time, and go 'bubble fishing' as you go with a mixing stick (photo 4). This can take a little time but it is worth the trouble.

USING HEAT

Bubble fishing in poured resin is a time-consuming process, so some people choose to use heat as a much quicker way to eliminate bubbles. This is not something I do or recommend, but if you do decide to use heat on your resin you need to be very careful. Here's what you need to know:

- Overheating resin can cause an exothermic reaction, and if the resin fuses with your moulds this will ruin them. Use heat sparingly and with extreme caution.

- Use a long clickable lighter or a heat gun on a low heat setting.

- For surface bubbles, pass the lighter flame or the heat from the heat gun over the top of the resin so that the heat pops the bubbles.

- Bubbles beneath the surface must be pulled to the surface using a mixing stick or a toothpick before you can pop them with your heat source.

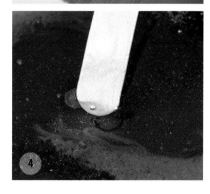

HOW TO LAYER

Layering is simple, but it can bring amazing depth and complexity to even the smallest piece. It also allows you to add colour to the background layer of a resin creation, making the foreground really stand out.

THE LAYERING PROCESS

When working with small moulds such as the jewellery pieces and hair accessory projects that I have included in this book, it would be difficult to fit more than two layers in. If you want to explore working with more layers, deeper moulds would be required – but the basic process described here would be the same.

1   Mix enough Coat-it resin to fill half your mould. Pour it in so that your mould is half full, then insert your flowers or embellishment of choice. Remember that the bottom of the mould is usually the front of your piece, although you should always double check this; if this is the case, place your insertions face down in the resin. Leave to partially cure.

2   When working in layers, the first layer of poured resin only needs to be touch dry before adding another layer, and with Coat-it resin this can be as soon as 5 or 6 hours after pouring. Timing is everything as you don't want to pour your second layer too quickly. If your first layer is still runny and you pour the second layer onto it and you are using flowers, they will float on the second layer rather than being fixed in place; however I have used metal insertions here, which are heavy, so they sit at the bottom of the mould.

3   With any other additions you make to the second layer, always keep your front/first layer in mind. Don't obstruct the view of the second layer insertions (if you add any) with, say, glitter that is too large or a colour pigment that is too strong.

4   Leave the second layer to fully cure before de-moulding - I like to leave the piece overnight.

HOW TO DE-MOULD

De-moulding can either be very easy or a little tricky; it all depends on the shape of the item! Most importantly your piece must be fully cured first, otherwise you risk distorting it. Curing times will vary depending on the resin brand but room temperature will have an effect too.

DE-MOULDING SIMPLE ITEMS

For small items that will easily pop out of the mould.

1   Start by peeling away the edges first. It's a very satisfying process!

2   Any excess resin can be snipped off with a pair of pliers or carefully sanded using the Rejuven8 Polishing Collection (see Tools & Materials: Resin crafting tools). Be warned, it is time-consuming to recapture the shine of the piece when it is first released from the mould, so do avoid it if you can.

DE-MOULDING ITEMS WITH CURVED EDGES OR 3D SHAPES

For large items such as cubes or spheres with a small opening.

1   Fill a small bowl with warm, soapy water and submerge the piece to be de-moulded.

2   Pull the sides of the mould away slightly so that the water can get in between the mould and the resin. This should make the de-moulding process a lot easier.

1

1

2

2

HOW TO DRY FLOWERS

Flowers and other botanicals, including moss, leaves, seeds and even tiny mushrooms, make great resin insertions. While these can be bought ready to use, it is very easy to prepare your own. Let's explore the drying options.

TRADITIONAL FLOWER PRESS

A traditional flower press will flatten the flower, but it is still a popular choice for many. However, you will need to be very patient as drying flowers in this way can take many weeks, even if they are small.

The flower press has layers of cardboard and absorbent paper sandwiched between two cover boards, usually wooden, which are all held together with wingnut bolts at each corner of the press. Unscrew the bolts and remove the top cover layer to gain access to the cardboard/paper layers.

Place your flowers in between the sheets of absorbent paper, which are sandwiched between the cardboard layers, arranging the flowers so that they do not overlap each other. Restack the cardboard layers, then replace the bolts at each corner, screwing them on as tightly as you can. Note that the press may need to be tightened as the flowers dry, so do check every few days.

MICROWAVEABLE FLOWER PRESS

The use of a microwaveable flower press will speed things up considerably! Place the flowers in between the fabric sheets and, following the instructions given, heat in the microwave in short 15-second bursts. The flowers will be pressed and dried in a matter of minutes.

Always ensure that the botanicals are completely dry or they will rot and turn brown over time.

SILICA SAND

My preferred drying method is the silica sand method, as it allows you to preserve the colour and shape of the whole flower. As well as the silica sand, you will need an airtight container for drying the flowers in.

1   Pour a thin layer of silica sand in the bottom of the tub, then place your flowers on this and slowly pour more sand over the top. Make sure you get into all the crevices of the flower, especially if it has a lot of petals, as it must be fully covered with the sand to ensure that all of its moisture is drawn out.

2   Different-sized flowers will need to be left in the sand for varying amounts of time: small flowers, such as forget-me-nots, only need a couple of days, whereas larger flowers, such as roses, can take several weeks. Check on your flowers to see how things are going, daily for small flowers and every three days for larger ones. Once completely dry, they will feel paper-like and lightweight.

3   Carefully remove dried flowers from the sand using a fine sieve or mesh. If sand remains on the flowers use a soft brush to remove it, but be careful – they will be very delicate and prone to breaking.

Store flowers until you are ready to use them in an airtight box and add a teaspoon of sand to it.

1

2

3

HOW TO MAKE A CUSTOM MOULD

Learning how to make a custom mould helps you to make resin pieces that are exclusive to you, an essential skill for those hoping to turn their resin crafting into a business. Here's an easy method you can try at home.

YOU WILL NEED

· Laser-cut acrylic blank (see step 1)
· Plastic cup or container
· Sticky back plastic sheet
· Hot glue gun
· Nitrile gloves
· Liquid silicone
· Mica powder (optional)
· Mixing cup and stick
· Small pair of scissors

1 The first job is to make a 'blank' around which the silicone mould is formed. I design mine with a digital drawing software program, then I send the PNG file to a laser cutting company to cut it to the size I want it to be, from 3mm (⅛in) Perspex (Plexiglas) with engraved details 1mm (less than ¹⁄₁₆in) deep. Remember: if you want a shiny mould, your blank needs to be shiny too!

2 Then you need to create a 'wall' to contain the liquid silicone around the blank. For small designs, cut the top half off a plastic cup and place it on a sheet of sticky back plastic with the top edge facing down (for bigger designs, use the top half of a plastic container, such as a sandwich box).

3 Run your hot glue gun all the way around the outside edge of the plastic cup to seal it to the sticky back plastic sheet, making sure there are no gaps at all that silicone can seep out of in step 6.

4 Place your blank in the centre of your walled-off area so that the side with the engraved details is facing up.

5 Pop on your nitrile gloves ready to mix a batch of liquid silicone: this comes in two parts that are usually combined in a 1:1 ratio. You'll need enough to submerge your blank, with a depth of about 1cm (⅜in) above it. Mix slowly until thoroughly combined, making sure you scrape the sides and the bottom of your cup well. This takes at least 3 minutes.

6 Pour the mixed silicone over your blank and leave it to fully cure. Different brands of silicone have different curing times and often cure faster in a warm room, so this can take anywhere from 1 to 4 hours!

7 Once fully cured, pull apart the plastic walls to release your mould, then push the blank out from the inside of the mould.

8 There is likely to be an uneven lip around the edge of your mould due to silicone shrinkage, so use a small pair of scissors to trim this away. Now your mould is ready to use.

You could make your blank out of polymer clay if you just want to get to grips with the technique, but the finish of the resin pieces will not be great in a polymer clay mould.

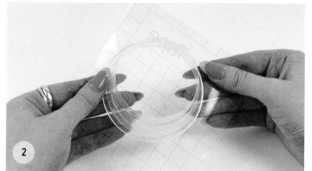

PROJECTS

PEARL-DROP FLOWER EARRINGS

The delicate beauty of small dried flowers – here I've chosen wood clematis – is preserved between two layers of resin to create a pair of elegant earrings. While different colours can be used for the two-layer technique, I've left most of the resin clear, utilizing just a little pearl pigment in the first layer to complement the pearl drops.

YOU WILL NEED

- Coat-it resin
- Pearl semi-transparent resin pigment
- Shapes mould
- Dried or pressed flowers of your choosing (see Techniques: How to dry flowers)
- Two electroplated pearl jump rings
- Two jump rings
- Two earring hooks
- Rotary tool or small hand drill and 2mm drill bit
- Two small pairs of jewellery pliers

1 Mix your Coat-it resin and pour a first, thin, clear layer into your mould (see Techniques: How to mix and pour), saving a small amount to be used in step 3.

2 Now place your chosen dried flowers right side facing down in this first layer of clear resin (note that the bottom of your mould is the front of your piece).

3 Next, in a small cup, mix the pearl pigment into a small amount of the remaining clear resin.

4 Use a small mixing stick to pick up small amounts of the pearl pigment resin and swirl them around in the poured layer of clear resin, taking care not to disturb the position of the flower heads – a little goes a long way! Then leave to cure.

1

2

3

4

5 Once the first layer of resin has cured completely, it is time to mix and pour the final second layer. But first check if there any flower stems poking out of the resin, and if so, cut them off.

6 Mix your resin and leave it clear, then pour the second (back) layer into the mould. Leave to cure fully before de-moulding (see Techniques: How to de-mould).

7 Once de-moulded, drill a hole at the centre top of each of your resin pieces.

8 Using the pliers, attach the pearl joiners between the earring hooks and the resin pieces with jump rings (see Tools & Materials: Jewellery essentials). Your earrings are now ready to wear!

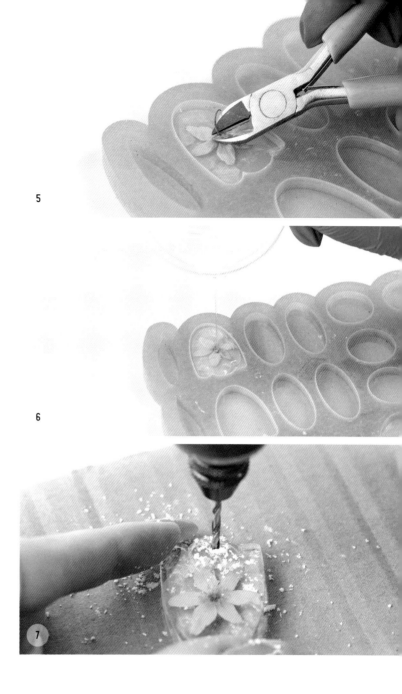

5

6

7

8

INTO THE FOREST PENDANT

For this wonderful woodland-themed necklace, I have created a forest idyll forever suspended in resin, using tiny mushrooms, delicate forget-me-nots and a little moss, all dried to preserve their beauty. Set in an open-backed bezel frame, this enchanting scene can be admired from both sides. The perfect gift for nature lovers, this necklace can be personalized by choosing the intended recipient's favourite flowers.

YOU WILL NEED

- Coat-it resin
- Open-backed bezel of your choosing (piece shown is 28mm/$1^1/_{16}$in in diameter and 8mm/$^5/_{16}$in deep)
- Bezel tape
- Small crushed stones
- Small dried woodland flora: forget-me-nots, mushrooms, moss, etc (see Techniques: How to dry flowers)
- Necklace chain

1   We will be working in layers, so you need
    to start by mixing just enough Coat-it
    resin to fill half of your chosen bezel
    shape (see Techniques: How to mix and
    pour). Leave the mixed resin to de-bubble
    while you prepare your bezel shape
    for filling.

2   To create a temporary backing to hold
    the resin in place in the open-backed
    bezel, cut a small piece of bezel tape
    a little larger than the shape itself and
    lay it sticky side up on a hard, flat work
    surface; avoid touching the tape where
    your bezel will be placed, as this will leave
    fingerprints on the back of your finished
    pendant. Place your bezel on the tape
    and push down firmly to avoid any resin
    leaking out in step 3.

3   Once you have removed any bubbles
    (see Techniques: How to avoid bubbles),
    pour a thin layer of resin into the bezel
    to a depth of around 1mm (1/16in) (see
    Techniques: How to mix and pour).

4   We are working from back to front here,
    so the first layer you put down in the
    resin is the back of the scene you will be
    creating. Add the small crushed stones
    and push them to the bottom using a
    mixing stick.

*Open-backed bezels come in
a variety of different shapes,
including circles, ovals, squares
and hearts. Designed to be viewed
from both sides, they are ideal for
botanical jewellery.*

5   Next, carefully place your chosen dried woodland flora in the resin: I've used forget-me-nots as they're so small that they fit into the bezel perfectly, along with moss (any lichen would look lovely) and tiny mushrooms.

6   Once you are happy with the arrangement of your botanical pieces, leave to cure.

7   Once the first layer of resin has cured, it is time to mix and pour the final, second layer of Coat-it resin, enough to fill the bezel up to the top. Then leave to cure overnight.

8   Once the resin has fully cured, remove the tape from the back of the bezel. Thread the pendant onto your chosen chain and your necklace is complete.

If the bezel tape leaves a sticky residue, it can easily be removed with a cloth and acetone.

FORGET-ME-NOT NECKLACE

This dainty necklace captures the delicate details of pressed forget-me-not flowers, which have been beautifully preserved by coating them in a careful amount of resin. Their cool blue tones are perfectly complemented by an elegant silver chain. I have chosen to keep my piece very minimal with just three flowers, but you can always add more, or even another type of flower in between, or perhaps some freshwater pearl drops.

YOU WILL NEED

- Coat-it resin
- Silicone mat
- Pressed forget-me-nots (see Techniques: How to dry flowers)
- Necklace chain
- Small jump rings
- Rotary tool or small hand drill and 0.6mm drill bit
- Two small pairs of jewellery pliers

1 Mix a small amount of Coat-it resin, then leave to de-bubble while you prepare your work surface.

2 We will be working on a silicone mat so make sure it is nice and clean, removing any fluff with a piece of tape.

3 Place the forget-me-not flowers on the silicone mat, spacing them about 2.5cm (1in) apart.

4 Use your mixing stick to place a small droplet of resin on each flower, carefully spreading it to cover the petals. Then leave to cure.

Forget-me-nots are delicate flowers, so you will need to be gentle when working with them. Prepare a few extras in case of accidents!

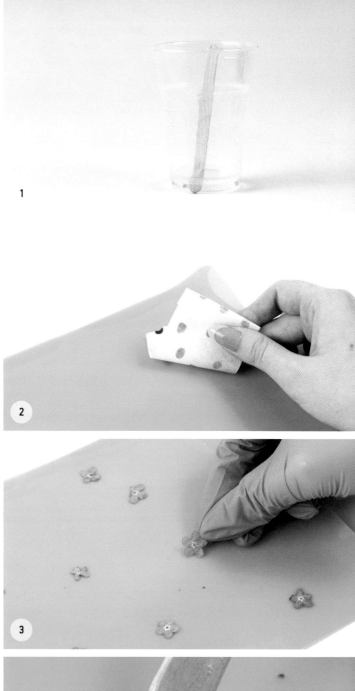

5   Once fully cured, gently peel the flowers off the mat and flip them over one at a time. Mix a small amount of Coat-it resin and repeat step 4 to coat the back of each flower, then leave to cure once again.

6   Once fully cured, gently peel the coated flowers off the mat. They are now ready to work with. Start by drilling a small hole at the base of one of the petals on each of the flowers.

7   Using the pliers, attach each of the flowers to the necklace chain with a small jump ring (see Tools & Materials: Jewellery essentials), spacing them evenly apart. Now your necklace is ready to wear!

For my design, I have added just three flowers to the chain – but of course you can attach more should you wish!

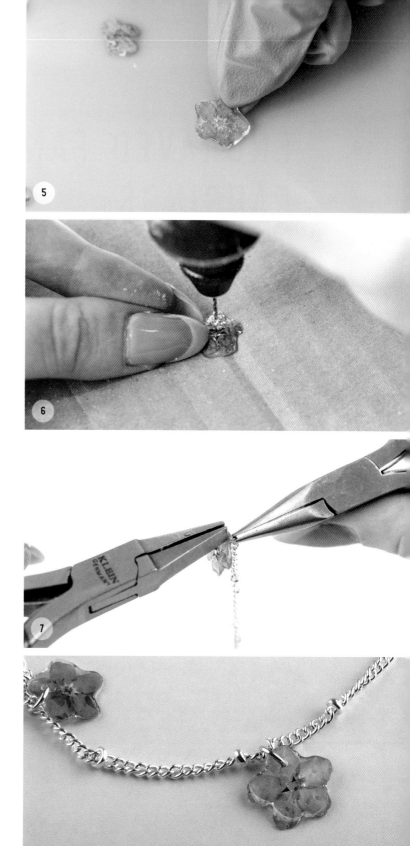

ENGRAVED FAN EARRINGS

These beautiful earrings have been inspired by the hand-painted floral patterns often seen on Japanese silk fans. Tiny pressed flowers have been preserved in clear resin, then backed with a bold red layer. The mould used has an engraved design that is highlighted with gold acrylic paint, protected beneath a shiny resin top coat. Luxurious silk tassel charms add dramatic flair.

YOU WILL NEED

- Coat-it resin
- Bright red resin pigment
- Japanese fan mould (see Suppliers)
- Small pressed flowers (see Techniques: How to dry flowers)
- Gold acrylic paint
- Liquid latex
- Large red silk tassel charms
- Large gold jump rings
- Earring posts and backs

- Rotary tool or small hand drill and 1.8mm drill bit
- Two small pairs of jewellery pliers
- Superglue

1   The design of the mould creates engraved lines within the first layer of resin, which we will be highlighting after de-moulding, but not until step 6! To begin, mix a small amount of Coat-it resin, enough to fill half of each section of the mould, and pour it in (see Techniques: How to mix and pour).

2   Place the small flowers right side facing down in this first layer of clear resin (note that the bottom of your mould is the front of your piece). Leave to cure.

3   Once the first layer of resin has cured, it is time to mix and pour the second pigmented layer. Mix a small amount of Coat-it resin, enough to fill the rest of each section of the mould, then add a small amount of the bright red pigment and mix well.

4   Pour the pigmented resin into the mould, filling it up to the top. Leave to cure.

Small pressed flowers work best for this project, as the mould is just 3mm (1/8in) deep.

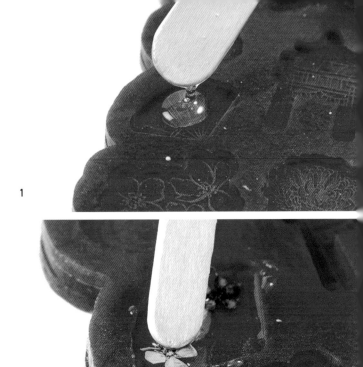

1

2

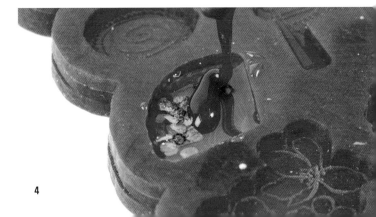

3

4

5 Once fully cured, it is time to de-mould the fan shapes (see Techniques: How to de-mould); this will reveal the engraved lines on the front of each of your resin pieces.

6 Rub gold acrylic paint into the engraved lines using your finger (a paintbrush can be helpful, too). Leave to dry.

7 Once dry, use a damp cloth to rub the excess paint off the resin pieces to reveal the gold fan design. Then wipe off any remaining moisture from the shapes with a dry cloth.

8 A final thin layer of clear resin needs to be applied to seal in the gold lines. Mix a small amount of Coat-it resin and set aside for 15 minutes to allow it to thicken.

When adding the gold paint, don't use too much; it's best to start with a small amount.

9   While the resin is thickening, prepare the fan shapes by brushing the base and edges of each resin piece with liquid latex. This will ensure that when you apply the final resin layer in step 10, it remains on the top of the design only, protecting the sides and base of each piece from any accidental spills.

10   Use the slightly thickened resin to add a thin top coat to each piece, applying it with a mixing stick, to give your earrings a smooth, professional look. Leave to cure.

11   Once fully cured, drill a small hole at the base of each fan. Then, using the pliers, attach the red silk tassels to the resin pieces with large gold jump rings (see Tools & Materials: Jewellery essentials).

12   Superglue an earring post onto the back of each earring and allow the adhesive to dry completely before wearing.

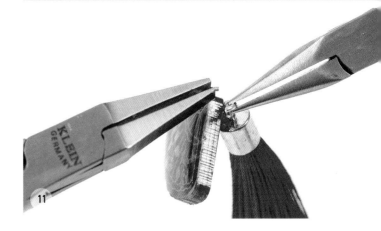

SHIMMERING ABSTRACT COASTER

This little coaster brings a subtle hint of glamour to coffee time. Made using heatproof resin for maximum practicality, the abstract flower design is formed in delicate pale pastel tones of blue and green, while gold and copper glitter and metallic foils add that all-important shimmer. It's guaranteed you'll have so much fun you'll want to make a matching set!

YOU WILL NEED

· Heatproof resin
· Resin pigments: sky blue and peppermint
· Square lipped coaster mould
· Eco glitter: gold and copper
· Dinky autumn mix (tiny metal leaf flakes)

1 We will be working in two layers for this project. For the first layer, mix enough heatproof resin to fill half of your mould (see Techniques: How to mix and pour). Now pour a small amount of the resin into two additional cups; these will have pigment added to them in step 2, but leave the majority of the resin clear in the original cup.

2 Mix peppermint pigment into one of the cups that contains a small amount of resin and sky blue pigment into the other, then set aside.

3 Pour the clear resin in the remaining cup into the coaster mould and leave for about 15 minutes.

4 Now it's time to complete the first layer by pouring in the pigmented resins. Starting with the peppermint pigment, pour it over the clear resin in a bold flower shape.

Before adding the first of the pigmented resins, carefully check the clear resin layer for bubbles and remove (see Techniques: How to avoid bubbles). If you don't, they will be very noticeable in this transparent design.

5 Repeat step 4 to pour a bold sky blue flower on top of the peppermint flower, offsetting the petals if you can and leaving a little resin in the cup.

6 Mix a small amount of gold glitter into the remaining sky blue resin, which turns it into more of a light olive green. Now pour this over your design – I've done mine in a sort of star shape. The first layer is now complete. Leave to cure.

7 Once the first layer has cured, it's time to add the final layer. Mix enough heatproof resin to fill the rest of the mould and pour almost all of it into the back of the mould, leaving a small amount in your cup for adding the final decoration.

8 Mix the gold and copper glitter and the metal leaf flakes into the small amount of resin remaining in the cup, then pour this into the mould, once again in a bold flower shape. As we are using the resin straight away rather than leaving it to thicken, it will spread out further this time. Leave it to fully cure before de-moulding (see Techniques: How to de-mould).

Don't use the coaster for hot drinks for at least 28 days, as the heatproof qualities of the resin need time to mature. Refer to the manufacturer's instructions for product-specific details.

5

6

7

8

FAUX MARBLE COASTERS

In this project, plain MDF blanks are transformed into luxurious marble-effect coasters. Use alcohol inks to mimic the natural beauty of this hard-wearing stone in any of its many colourways - I've gone for a rose quartz and a green onyx. Then cover your 'art' with a heatproof resin to extend the use of your coasters, so that they are suitable for morning lattes as well as evening cocktails.

YOU WILL NEED

- Heatproof resin
- Alcohol inks in colours of your choosing
- MDF coaster blanks
- White acrylic paint and paintbrush

1   First you will need to prime the MDF
    blanks by painting them with two layers
    of white acrylic paint, allowing the paint
    time to dry in between coats.

2   Once the second layer of acrylic paint
    has dried, you can begin to create your
    faux marble effect. Start by researching
    the type of marble you would like to
    recreate, then gather together the alcohol
    ink colours you will need. I have chosen
    pink, purple and copper to create a rose
    quartz, and green, yellow and gold for a
    green onyx.

3   To create a faux marble effect, drop the
    inks onto your primed coaster one at
    a time.

4   Swap between your chosen colours to
    create your desired effect.

1

2

3

4

5 Remember, no squirting or you'll use too much ink. The inks will spread, so do use them sparingly.

6 Add the metallic colour last, so that it sits on the surface and creates a beautiful shimmer.

7 Once you are happy with the effect you have achieved, leave the inks to dry for a minimum of an hour.

8 Pour a small amount of mixed heatproof resin into the middle of the coaster and use a small mixing stick to spread it evenly to cover the surface right up to the edge. Leave to cure. This can take up to 28 days but drying times will vary according to the product used, so always check the manufacturer's instructions.

The alcohol inks can have quite a strong smell, so place the coasters in a box and put them out of the way to dry.

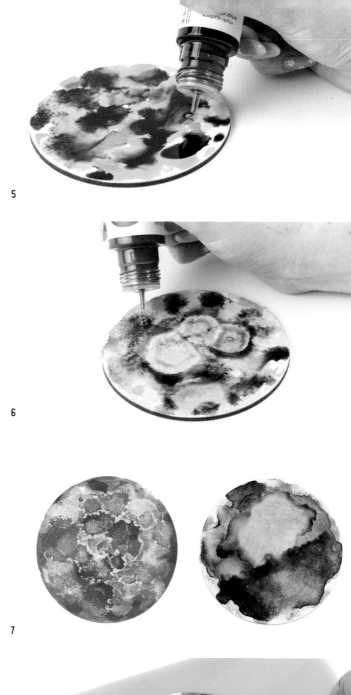

5

6

7

8

ANIMAL PRINT MAKE-UP TRAY

Take a walk on the wild side with this glitzy dressing table tray, perfect for keeping all your make-up favourites to hand. It's also a great way to try out some of the wonderful range of additions available for your resin, from pigments to copper foil and glitter. The warm tones I have chosen are a perfect backdrop for the leopard-print decals, which are protected by pouring on a final thin layer of clear resin.

YOU WILL NEED

- Coat-it resin
- Copper glitter
- Resin pigments: white, black and rich brown
- Copper leaf
- Leopard-print vinyl decals
- XL tray mould

1   Begin by mixing your Coat-it resin. You'll need a lot to fill the tray mould and it is safest to mix it in several cups rather than as one big batch (for more about mixing large quantities of resin, see Techniques: How to mix and pour).

2   Divide your resin equally into four cups. To each cup add one of your insertions – copper glitter, white pigment, black pigment, rich brown pigment – and mix well.

3   Using a soft brush, dust some copper leaf across the inside of your tray mould.

4   Pour your mixed resins into the mould, working one at a time. You can work diagonally in strips as I have done, or you can pour in more random patches if you choose to. I started in one corner with the rich brown resin, then added white alongside, followed by black.

1

2

3

4

5 I continued with a wide central strip of copper glitter resin.

6 Then I added another strip of rich brown resin, then a strip of black, finishing with white to fill the mould. Once you have filled your tray, leave it to cure.

7 Once fully cured, de-mould your tray (see Techniques: How to de-mould). Now you can decorate the tray with your leopard-print vinyl decals, working across one corner of the design. Apply them to the bottom of the tray only, not on the sides or the edges.

8 Mix a small amount of Coat-it resin, enough to cover the bottom of the tray, and pour on a thin layer to seal the decals into the design. Leave to fully cure before putting your tray to use.

The pigmented resins naturally flow into each other if you have poured quickly and the resin hasn't thickened too much. If necessary, you can encourage the blending by using a mixing stick.

OCEAN WAVES SERVING TRAY

Even if you live in the middle of the city, you can bring a hint of a sea breeze to your dining room table with this beautiful server. Carefully curating your coastal world on the edge of the board allows you to safely serve drinks and snacks on the area not covered with the breaking waves resin design.

YOU WILL NEED

- Coat-it resin
- Medium to large wooden serving board
- Resin pigments: dark blue, light blue and white
- Selection of small shells, pebbles and textured sands
- Low-tack masking tape
- Protective mat or sheet
- Small cups
- Heat gun

1 You will be working at one corner of the
   serving board on the top of the board
   only. To protect the edge and base of the
   board at this corner, apply a low-tack
   masking tape, pushing it down well for
   a tight seal and extending it by at least
   2.5cm (1in) across the base of the board.

2 Place a protective mat or sheet that
   is larger than your board on your work
   surface. Take several small cups of the
   same height and place them on top of
   the protective mat or sheet. Now sit the
   board on top of the cups so that it is
   elevated, to ensure that any resin overspill
   is able to run off the edge and onto the
   protective surface below.

3 Mix the Coat-it resin (see Techniques: How
   to mix and pour) and divide it equally into
   three other cups, leaving a small amount
   of clear resin in your original cup.

4 Mix one of your pigments into each of
   these three cups. You should now have
   three cups of pigmented resin (white, light
   blue and dark blue) plus one cup with a
   small amount of clear resin in it.

5 Starting with the dark blue resin, begin to pour it on to fill the prepared corner of the board, working from the wider edge and slowly getting closer to the corner. The resin is likely to run off the edge on its own, but you can encourage it with your mixing stick if necessary.

6 Then pour the light blue resin along the inside edge of the dark blue resin.

7 Use a mixing stick to smudge the line where the two colours meet to effectively blend the colours together. It can help here to add small droplets of clear resin.

8 Once the dark and blue layers are blended, pour a line of clear resin along the edge of the light blue resin.

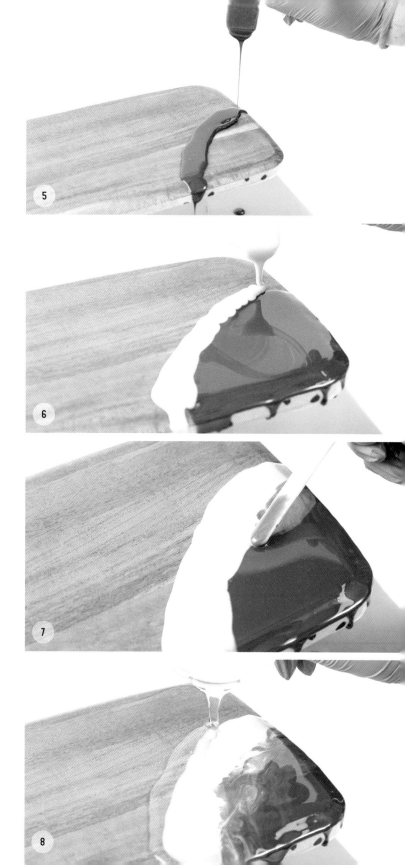

9   Now pour a thin line of white resin along the edge of the clear resin.

10 Then, starting at the wider edge and using the heat gun to blow the white resin towards the corner, push and move it into the blues to create a gentle wave-like effect. Make sure that you hold the heat gun quite far away at first, going closer to the piece if required.

11 Pour a thin line of clear resin next to the white wave line and start to create your 'beach' by applying sand along this line. I have used three different textured sands from very fine to a little bit chunkier. The clear resin acts as your 'glue', so add a little more on top of the sand if it is necessary to hold it in place.

12 Finally, add a few small pebbles and shells where the wave breaks onto the shoreline, then leave your decorated board to fully cure.

The textured sands and shells I have used are sourced from craft suppliers, but you could collect sand from your favourite beach to make it even more personal to you.

13 You may decide that you like the board as it looks once it has fully cured and if so, all you need do is to remove the tape and it's ready to use. However, if you would like to achieve a more dramatic breaking surf effect, it's time to add more detail. Start by mixing up more Coat-it resin.

14 Working **only** on the sea part of the design (not including the beach), pour the clear resin over three quarters of the sea area, from the wider area towards the corner, making sure you retain a little clear resin in the cup. Now add white pigment to the retained clear resin, then pour a thin line of white resin along the edge of the clear resin.

15 Now use your heat gun to move the white resin to create the wave-like effects. Leave to cure.

16 Repeat steps 14 and 15 as many times as you like until you are happy with the effect. Then leave once more to fully cure.

Always work with caution when using a heat source, and don't forget to remove the tape from the board before using it!

GALAXY SIDE TABLE

This design is out of this world, inspired as it is by the swirling galaxies of outer space! Celestial hues are mixed into clear resin, and texture is added with a variety of embellishing materials, from glitter and sand to teeny, tiny glass beads. A little hand-drawn pen detailing completes the stellar effect, then your cosmic masterpiece is protected and preserved beneath a heatproof resin layer.

YOU WILL NEED

- Coat-it resin
- Heatproof resin
- Resin pigments: deep sea blue, deep plum and black
- Black ultrafine glitter
- Black sand
- Silver glitter
- Teeny, tiny glass beads
- Paint pens
- Metal side table with lipped edge
- 400-grit sandpaper

1 First, to prepare the top surface of your metal table, you will need to sand it to create a key that the resin coating can adhere to. If you don't sand, you risk your resin centrepiece popping out if the table if knocked! Wipe the table clean.

2 You'll need a lot of resin to fill the tray mould: mix it up in several cups rather than as one big batch (for more about mixing large quantities of resin, see Techniques: How to mix and pour). Divide the resin equally into four cups.

3 Leaving one cup of clear resin (in case you need to mix more of any of the pigmented resins as you work), mix your chosen pigments for creating the galaxy effect into each of the other three cups, to give you one cup of deep sea blue resin, one cup of plum resin, and one cup of resin that has black pigment and ultrafine black glitter in it.

4 It's time to start pouring your mixed pigmented resins into the tray created by the lipped edge of the table.

1

2

3

4

5 As you pour in each colour, try to make sure that the blue and purple are near or next to each other.

6 When you have poured your coloured resins into the table tray, carefully tilt it to evenly cover the surface. This helps to ensure that you do not overfill the tray, and you should only add more resin after encouraging it to spread over as much of the area as possible in this way.

7 Use a small mixing stick to blend the edges of the blue and purple colours together and slightly into the black too.

8 Now scatter on the silver glitter, remembering that a little goes a long way – it's so fine, you'll find it sits in the surface nicely. Apply it in a controlled way, in two bands, to create the stripes.

When pouring your coloured pigmented resins and adding the glitter, always work slowly . . . remember, it is much easier to add more than it is to take it away!

9 Scatter on the black sand and teeny, tiny glass beads in a concentrated area; applying them near the silver glitter will create areas of high detail. Now leave the resin-coated table to cure.

10 Once the resin has hardened, you can use a white paint pen to draw on little white dots to resemble stars, or any other finishing details in colour pens of your choosing (any light pastel colour, particularly yellow, would look nice). Leave to dry for at least an hour before applying the final layer of heatproof resin.

11 Mix your heatproof resin and pour on a layer about 5mm (¼in) thick (see Techniques: How to mix and pour).

12 Check the surface for bubbles and fish them out with a small mixing stick (see Techniques: How to avoid bubbles). Leave to cure before using your table. This can take up to 28 days but drying times will vary according to the product used, so always check the manufacturer's instructions.

Heatproof resin can take several weeks to cure, so do remember to follow the manufacturer's guidance before placing hot drinks on the surface.

MOTHER-OF-PEARL MERMAID'S COMB

This must-have haircare accessory makes the perfect present for a beach-loving friend. It is created in two layers. The natural beauty of the mother-of-pearl pieces used in the first clear resin layer are perfectly complemented by the pigmented resins, a delicate pearl and a bubble gum pink, that twist and flow into each other as the second layer is poured.

YOU WILL NEED

- Resin pigments: bubble gum and pearl
- Comb mould
- Mother-of-pearl pieces
- Coat-it resin
- Toothpick

1 Start by mixing your first batch of Coat-it resin, enough to fill just under half of the comb mould. Refer to Techniques: How to mix and pour for more instruction, but in this instance, I would recommend first warming up part A by standing it in a jug of hot water. This will give the mixed resin a thinner consistency to ensure that it will flow a lot more easily into the fine teeth area of the comb mould.

2 Pour the resin into your mould slowly and encourage it into the teeth of the comb using the toothpick. Make sure you remove any bubbles, particularly from the teeth of the comb (see Techniques: How to avoid bubbles).

3 Select your pieces of mother-of-pearl and place them face down in the comb mould. I have chosen to overlap mine so that they really stand out, but you can add fewer pieces if you prefer a more subtle look.

4 Use the mixing stick or toothpick to put some smaller pieces into the teeth of the comb. When you are happy with your shell arrangement, leave to cure.

Shell pieces are available in lots of different colours, so check out your options. You can choose very tiny whole seashells if you prefer.

1

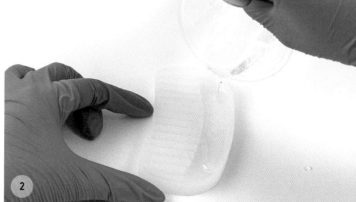

2

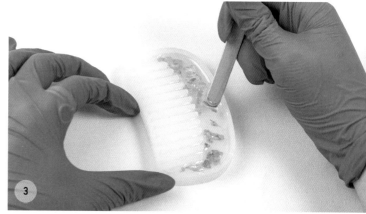

3

4

5 Now mix enough Coat-it resin to fill the rest of the comb mould and divide it equally between two cups. Mix a small amount of bubble gum pigment into the resin in one cup and pearl pigment into the other.

6 Now pour the pigmented resins into the mould, a little of each at a time until it is full, using the toothpick to 'encourage' the pigmented resins into the teeth of the comb. Leave to cure.

7 Once it has fully cured, de-mould your comb (see Techniques: How to de-mould). You may find slight resin overflow on the teeth of the comb; if so, carefully clip it off with a pair of small pliers. Then your comb is ready to use or to gift!

The large area at the top of the comb mould means it would be ideally suited to botanical decorations too, should you fancy making another.

5

6

7

GOLDEN FLORAL KEY RING

With its delicate florals and luxurious gold leaf insertions, this delightful key ring would make the perfect house-warming gift. For a very personal offering, choose an alphabet mould – there are so many different lettering styles to choose from, but I couldn't resist selecting a Sixties font as the pretty preserved daisies and bright yellow resin backing bring to mind the Summer of Love.

YOU WILL NEED

- Coat-it resin
- Key ring mould
- Dried daisies (see Techniques: How to dry flowers)
- Gold leaf
- Yellow resin pigment
- Key ring chain
- Large jump ring
- Rotary tool or small hand drill and 2mm drill bit
- Two small pairs of jewellery pliers

1   If your chosen key ring mould is quite
    small, cut your daisy flowers to fit into it
    first, then put the cut flower pieces aside.

2   Mix the Coat-it resin and pour the first,
    thin, clear layer in your mould (see
    Techniques: How to mix and pour).

3   Place the daisy pieces right side facing
    down into this first layer of clear resin
    (note that the bottom of your mould is
    the front of your piece).

4   Now add the gold leaf, then leave to cure.

5 Once the first layer of resin has cured, it is time to mix and pour the final, second layer. Mix a small amount of Coat-it resin, add the yellow pigment and mix well.

6 Pour the pigmented resin into the mould, filling it up to the top.

7 Leave it to fully cure, then de-mould (see Techniques: How to de-mould).

8 Drill a hole at the top of your de-moulded resin letter shape ready, then use the jewellery pliers to attach the key ring chain to it with a large jump ring (see Tools & Materials: Jewellery essentials).

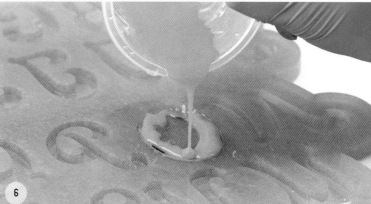

KEEPSAKE PHOTO KEY RING

Any photo can be carefully preserved in resin for lasting memories, and what better way to display them than in a key ring, to be enjoyed every day. Small but perfectly formed, these tiny creations make the ideal new home gift, of course, but they are so easy to make that they would be ideal as wedding favours too.

YOU WILL NEED

- Coat-it resin
- Key ring mould
- Small photo (to fit your mould)
- Pressed flowers of your choosing (see Techniques: How to dry flowers)
- Key ring
- Large jump ring
- Laminator and laminating sheets
- Rotary tool or small hand drill and 2mm drill bit
- Two small pairs of jewellery pliers

1 When selecting your photo, it is important to make sure that it will fit inside your mould; cut it 2mm (¹⁄₁₆in) smaller than the mould, as you need to allow for a small border of laminate in step 2.

2 Laminate your photograph, then trim to the shape of the photograph leaving a 2mm (¹⁄₁₆in) border of laminate all round. (If you cut the laminate edge too close to your photograph, the resin will seep inside.)

3 Mix enough Coat-it resin to fill half of your mould and pour it in. It's important with such a small piece to remove any bubbles (see Techniques: How to avoid bubbles).

4 Carefully place your chosen pressed flowers right side facing down in the resin, then lay your photograph right side facing down on top (note that the bottom of your mould is the front of your piece). Leave to cure.

It is important to laminate your photograph to prevent it from absorbing the resin, otherwise the ink will bleed and the photo will be ruined.

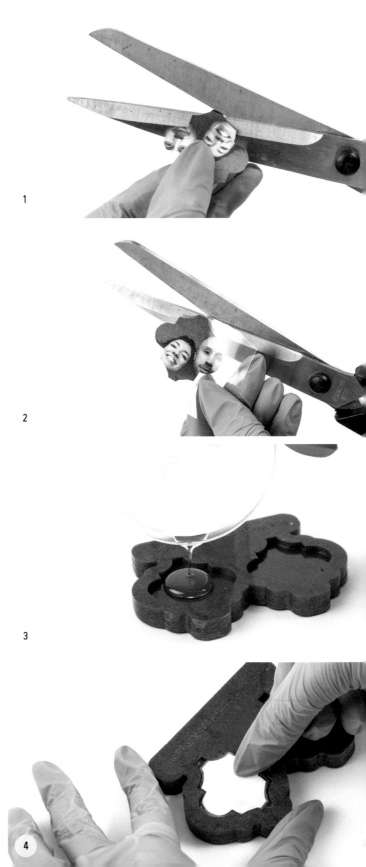

1

2

3

4

5   Now mix enough resin to fill the rest of
    the mould. If you want, you could add
    a pigment to the resin to colour it, but I
    have chosen to keep my back layer clear.
    Pour the resin into the mould and leave
    to cure.

6   Once it has fully cured, de-mould your
    key ring shape (see Techniques: How to
    de-mould).

7   Drill a medium-sized hole at the top of
    your resin piece.

8   Using the jewellery pliers, attach the
    key ring chain to the resin piece with a
    large jump ring (see Tools & Materials:
    Jewellery essentials).

*To make your photo key ring even
more special, substitute something
more personal for the flowers – a
lock of a loved one's hair, perhaps?*

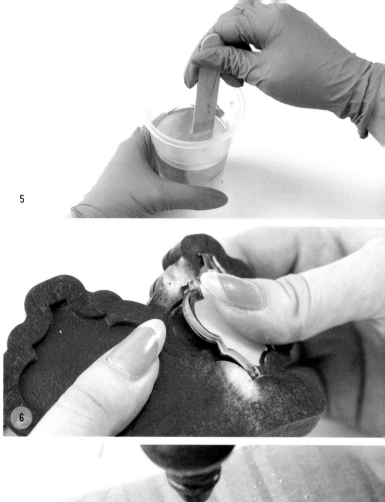

SUPER SPARKLY HAIR CLIP

A glitzy little clip is the perfect addition to any party outfit. With its opal flake decoration, this hair accessory is not only beyond pretty but it's really practical too, featuring an alligator clip fitting that keeps your hair out of your eyes while you are busy getting those dance moves down. Why not make more in different colours? You won't regret it!

YOU WILL NEED

- Coat-it resin
- Opal flake glitter
- Pearl pigment
- Hair clip mould
- Alligator hair clip approx. 7cm (3in) long
- Superglue

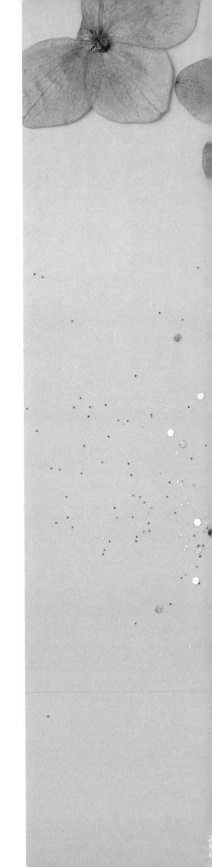

1 Mix enough Coat-it resin to fill your hair clip mould (see Techniques: How to mix and pour), then add a lot of the opal flake glitter (see Tools & Materials: Insertions) and a small amount of pearl pigment and mix them in.

2 It is a good idea, especially due to the addition of such a large amount of glitter, to leave the resin to rest for about 10 minutes before pouring it, to let the bubbles come to the surface so that they can easily be removed (see Techniques: How to avoid bubbles).

3 Pour the resin into the hair clip mould and leave to cure.

4 Once fully cured, de-mould your hair clip resin piece (see Techniques: How to de-mould).

5 To attach an alligator clip to the back of the resin piece, first spread a little superglue onto the top of the clip.

6 Then press the glued surface of the clip onto the back of your resin piece and leave to dry overnight. Next day your clip will be ready to wear.

5

6

You could leave the gluing on of the alligator clip until the next time you are making resin items, when you can use a little clear resin to fix it in place rather than superglue.

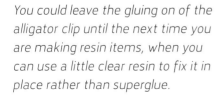

SHAKE IT UP HAIR CLIP

These cute kawaii-inspired hair clips are made using a shaker mould. There's no end of choice when it comes to filling the shaker sections of the mould, but I chose tiny rainbow slices of polymer clay along with one of my favourite types of glitter. Make sure you set aside a few days to make these as, although they are small, the process is time consuming.

YOU WILL NEED

- Coat-it resin
- Shaker hearts hair clip mould (see Suppliers)
- Resin pigments: bubble gum pink and Tresco blue
- Shaker insertions: fimo pieces and glitter of your choosing
- Acetate sheet
- UV resin and UV light
- Baby oil and applicator bottle with extra-fine tip

- Rotary tool or small hand drill and 1mm drill bit
- Metal hair clip and superglue

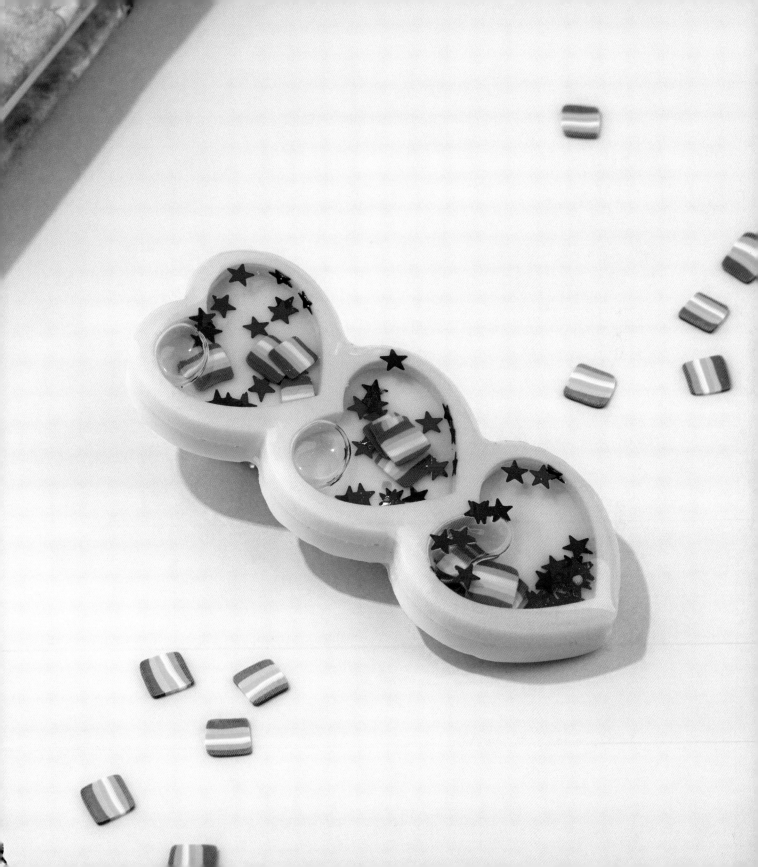

1 The resin is added to the mould in two layers, working from the front to the back. For the first layer, mix a small amount of Coat-it resin, enough to fill the deep sides of the hair clip mould (see Techniques: How to mix and pour). In the finished piece, this forms the outer edge of the heart sections.

2 Add a little pigment colour of your choosing into the clear resin: I have used a pretty bubble gum pink pigment.

3 Pour the bubble gum resin into the outer deep sides of the hair clip mould. Leave to cure.

4 Once the first section has cured, it is time to mix another small amount of Coat-it resin to fill the rest of the mould, colouring it with another pigment colour – this time I have used Tresco blue.

A shaker mould is a special type of mould that enables you to fill one or more sections within it with baby oil so that any insertions included will float free. There are many fun shapes and designs available.

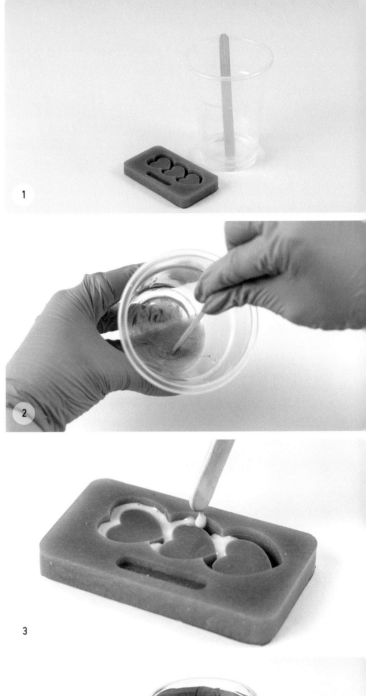

5 Pour the blue resin into the mould to form the back layer of the hair clip and then leave to cure.

6 Once fully cured, de-mould your piece (see Techniques: How to de-mould). This will reveal the heart-shaped cavities for your shaker insertions. Place your fimo pieces and glitter into each cavity, making sure that there is room for them to move around.

7 When your insertions are in place, lay your resin piece on top of the acetate sheet and trace around the outline.

8 Cut out the traced shape on the inside of the traced line, so that it is a little smaller than the resin piece.

Choosing what to fill your design with is half the fun. You could cast and use tiny resin shapes, for example, or utilize jewellery charms or beads.

5

6

7

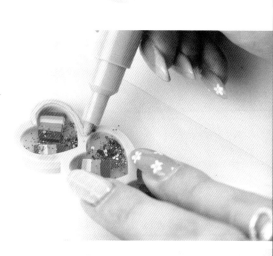

8

9 Squeeze a small amount of UV resin around the edge of the resin piece – if you accidentally use too much, use a mixing stick to lift it off. Lay your acetate on top and press it down, using a cloth to wipe away any excess that seeps out. Then leave it to cure under a UV light following the manufacturer's instructions (this will vary depending on the brand used, but won't be less than 3 minutes).

10 To make sure that the acetate is firmly attached, add a top layer of UV resin across the whole of the piece, then leave to cure once more under a UV light.

11 Once fully cured, it is time to complete the shaker cavities, by adding the baby oil so that the insertions can float freely. First you need to drill a tiny hole in the bottom edge of each of the heart cavities.

12 Insert the applicator tip of your bottle of baby oil into one of the holes and squeeze enough oil into the cavity to float the insertions. The pieces should move around within the oil, so be sure to leave a small air bubble to allow this to happen.

While I don't recommend UV resin for resin casting, it is perfect for quickly sealing the holes of the shaker sections once filled with baby oil.

9

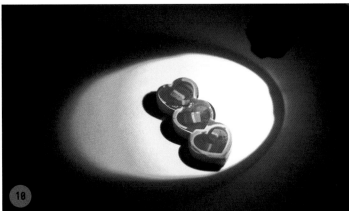

10

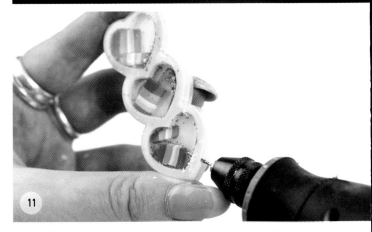

11

12

13 Cover the hole with a small amount of UV resin and cure under the UV light.

14 Repeat steps 12 and 13 for the remaining two cavities to complete the shaker element of your resin piece.

15 Use a little superglue to attach the finished shaker resin piece to the metal hair clip. Once the adhesive has dried, your clip will be ready to wear.

There are so many options when it comes to glitter. I love a chunky shaped glitter, but it all comes down to personal choice.

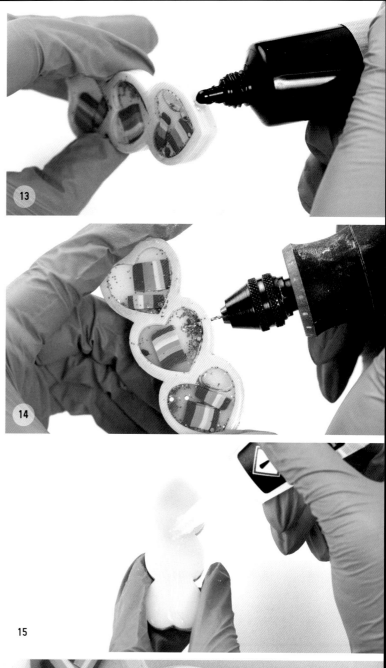

MAPLE LEAF PHONE CASE

I love autumn, when the leaves on the trees change to the most spectacular range of colours from golden yellows to rich browns, so I decided to capture the beauty of the season in a mobile phone case! I have used pressed maple leaves in a variety of shades alongside copper leaf for a harmonious pairing. Clear resin has been used to seal these insertions into a transparent shell to create the impression of delicately falling leaves.

YOU WILL NEED

- Coat-it resin
- Transparent mobile phone shell
- Copper leaf
- Pressed maple leaves (see Techniques: How to dry flowers)

1 Mix a small amount of Coat-it resin, then wait a little while for it to thicken – if it is too thin, it will run over the edge of the case and will be hard to manage.

2 Once the resin has thickened a little – this usually takes about 10 minutes – spread a thin layer onto the outside of your phone case using a mixing stick, covering all of the surface. Resin is self-levelling, so it will even out without help.

3 Now add little flecks of the copper leaf, using your mixing stick to put them in your preferred areas.

4 Then carefully lay your pressed maple leaves on top.

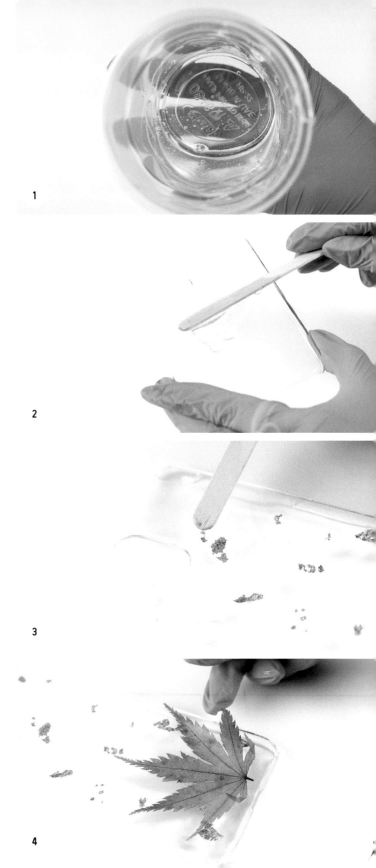

1

2

3

4

5   You can cut some of the leaves in half to cover more of the case if you wish to.

6   Once you are happy with the arrangement, leave to cure.

7   Once fully cured, you need to add a final thin layer of resin to seal and protect the decoration. Mix a small amount of Coat-it resin and leave to thicken slightly (see step 1). Add the top layer slowly, then leave to fully cure before inserting your mobile phone into the decorated shell.

5

6

Remember, it is easier to add more resin than it is to take it away when you have added too much!

7

POSY PAPERWEIGHT

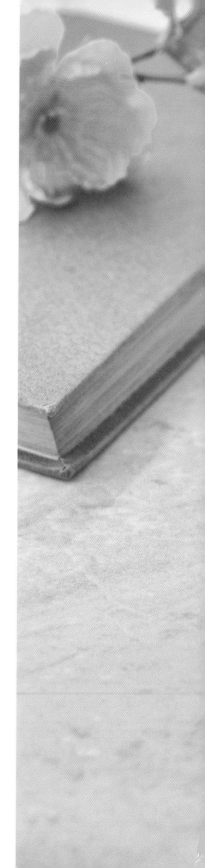

This paperweight is made using a deep pour resin, enabling you to capture the beauty of a mini bouquet of flowers forever, an ideal way to preserve blooms from special occasions such as birthdays and weddings. Deep pour resins take a little getting used to, as they have a longer working time and take so much longer to cure, but the results are worth it. I recommend drying flowers using silica sand to retain their colour and shape.

YOU WILL NEED

- Fill-it resin
- Paperweight mould
- Dried flowers (see Techniques: How to dry flowers).

1 We will be working in two layers, so start by mixing your first batch of Fill-it resin, just enough to fill a quarter of the paperweight mould (see Techniques: How to mix and pour). Leave the mixed resin to de-bubble.

2 Meanwhile, take your time to arrange your flowers in the paperweight mould. Remember that the bottom of the mould is the front of your finished piece, so arrange the flowers face down.

3 Once you have removed any bubbles (see Techniques: How to avoid bubbles), pour the resin into the mould. This first shallow layer of resin will 'anchor' your flowers in the mould and prevent them from floating, which is likely to happen in such a large piece.

4 Allow the first layer to start to cure, but be careful not to let it fully cure before mixing and pouring your final layer. When the flowers don't move and the resin has started to thicken and it is looking a little 'gluey', the right consistency has been achieved.

Timing is key and it is important to get it right to prevent a line appearing in your finished item.

5 When the resin has reached the correct consistency, mix enough Fill-it resin to fill the rest of the mould and carefully pour it in.

6 Leave it to fully cure before de-moulding (see Techniques: How to de-mould).

7 Once de-moulded, you may find that the bottom of the paperweight has a slight lip from shrinkage, or that the flowers have protruded slightly, creating a rough patch, and so it may prove necessary to sand off these imperfections. For advice on using the Rejuven8 Polishing Collection for this, see Tools & Materials: Resin crafting tools.

5

6

7

If the base of the paperweight is a little rough, you can either back it with felt or fix on little adhesive plastic feet to protect the surface it sits on.

CORAL HOOP EARRINGS

These super-shiny earrings have a colour and texture that catch the eye and demand to be noticed. I made mine using coral chips recycled from a vintage necklace, but it's easy to source faux coral chips that will have the same effect. Alternatively, use pieces of shell or semiprecious stones and choose your pigment colour to match.

YOU WILL NEED

- Coat-it resin
- Pastel peach resin pigment
- Hoop earring mould
- Recycled coral chips
- Earring posts and backs
- Rejuven8 Polishing Collection from Resin8 (see Tools & Materials: Resin crafting tools)
- Rotary tool or small hand drill and 1mm drill bit
- Two small pairs of jewellery pliers
- Superglue

1   Begin by mixing your Coat-it resin (see
    Techniques: How to mix and pour); hoop
    earrings are prone to bubbles, so take
    extra care to mix slowly. Divide your resin
    equally between two cups.

2   Mix pastel peach pigment into the resin in
    one cup and the coral pieces into the resin
    in the other cup, again mixing slowly.

3   With both cups close at hand, prepare to
    pour. Start by pouring the pigmented resin
    first into one end of the mould, but only a
    small amount.

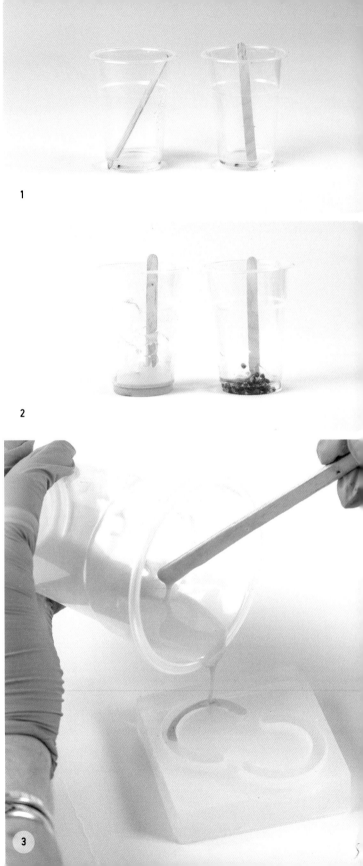

1

2

3

4 Now pour the clear resin with the added coral pieces into the other end of the mould.

5 Slowly add more of each of the resins until the mould is full. The pigmented resin will bleed into the clear resin slightly, so when you pour you may want to make the clear section larger that the pigmented section.

6 Leave the hoops to cure until fully hard, then de-mould (see Techniques: How to de-mould).

7 If there are large pieces of excess resin then clip it off with pliers before sanding, as this will save you some valuable sanding time.

When adding insertions to resin, watch out for air bubbles. Use a toothpick to coax out any that are trapped between the coral pieces.

8 While the fronts and sides of the hoops will be nice and shiny, the backs may have a slight dip or an edge that needs to be sanded smooth. Working with the lowest grit sandpaper (180) first, apply a tablespoon of water to the sandpaper and sand the back of your hoops until nice and flat, using a circular motion for a better finish.

9 Continuing in this way, use each sandpaper grit in numerical order – 180, 240, 400, 800, 1200, 2500 – do not miss any out! As you work your way up the grits, you should be able to feel the difference to the smoothness of the hoops as you finish working with each of the sandpapers.

10 By the time you are using the highest-grit sandpaper (2500), you can now feel how smooth to the touch the back of the hoops are. Wash them well in fresh water and dry with a towel.

11 At this stage the hoops look slightly dull but you will now use the abrasive paste and dark blue cloth to begin to coax out that shine.

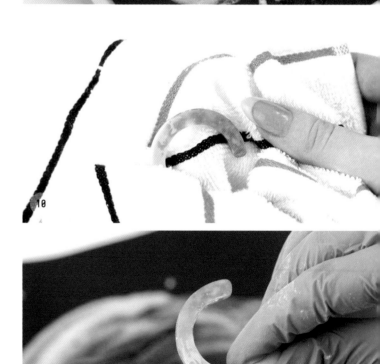

12 Apply two pumps of the abrasive paste onto the dark blue cloth, then rub the back of the hoops onto the paste in a circular motion for about 10 minutes.

13 Next, switching to the light blue cloth, spray the shine enhancer onto the cloth four times and once again rub the back of the hoops onto the cloth in a circular motion, to bring out the shine.

14 Now it's time to turn the shiny polished hoops into hoop earrings by attaching the earring posts. Using a rotary tool or a small hand drill with a 1mm drill bit attached, drill a short tunnel about 2mm (1/16in) deep into the end of each of the hoops, making sure you work at the end that does not have the coral pieces in it.

15 Use pliers to cut the flat circle off the earring posts so that you're left with just the pins. Using a small dot of superglue on the end of each pin, insert them into the drilled holes. Hold in place for 5 minutes, then leave to dry overnight.

It is very important to cure the hoops well before de-moulding. If your hoops are still slightly bendy, you will distort the shape when you sand them.

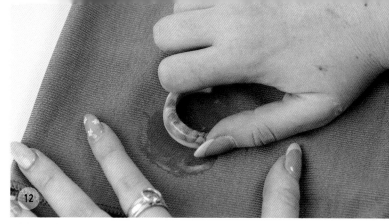

TROUBLESHOOTING

When you first start working with resin you may make mistakes and this is perfectly normal – I made lots of them myself and sometimes still do! I thought it would help if I compiled some handy tips and tricks to help you on your resin crafting journey. If you can't find the answer to your question here, there's lots of help on YouTube as well as mutual support on resin-based Facebook groups.

IS YOUR RESIN NOT SETTING WELL OR REMAINING BENDY WHEN IT SHOULD BE HARDENING?

- First, check the manufacturer's instructions. Did you cure it for the recommended time? Some resins take just 8 hours, while others take many days.

- Are you experiencing colder weather than usual? Resin will take longer to cure in a cooler environment. When temperatures are warmer than usual, however, your resin can cure very quickly and your working time will be minimized.

- Is the piece you are making very thin? Items that are only a few millimetres in thickness, such as a bookmark, will take longer to fully harden. It's important to leave thin items on a flat surface until they are fully cured to prevent them from bending.

- Did you get your measurements right when mixing your resin? You need to make sure you're measuring to the exact millilitre! If you don't, the chemical reaction will not work in the way that it is designed to and your resin will not fully cure.

- Are you scraping the very bottom of the cup as well as the sides as you mix your resin? This is really important as the resin needs to be mixed extremely well otherwise it will not cure.

- If your resin hasn't set, how can you remove it from your mould? Simply place it in a freezer bag and tightly secure to prevent resin leakage before placing it into your freezer. After a few hours the resin will have hardened so that you can pop it out of the mould and throw it away. If the mould remains sticky, use baby wipes to clean it.

ARE THERE BUBBLES IN YOUR RESIN?

- There are lots of ways that you can minimize bubbles occurring in your resin in the first place, and how you mix together the two parts, parts A and B, is very important. Work slowly, keep your mixing stick low in the cup, and always stir in the same direction.

- Before mixing, it can also help to slightly warm the resin part first by standing the part A bottle in a jug of warm water. This will make the resin runnier and therefore less prone to bubbles.

- You might want to leave the resin for a few minutes before pouring to give any bubbles a chance to rise to the surface, then remove them with a mixing stick.

- For more useful tips, see Techniques: How to mix and pour and How to avoid bubbles.

DOES YOUR RESIN LOOK CLOUDY IN THE BOTTLE?

- Do not panic! Your resin is just a little cold. Fill a jug with hot water and place the part A (resin) bottle in it and slowly it will become clear again.

ARE YOUR DRIED FLOWERS TURNING A DIFFERENT COLOUR IN THE RESIN?

- If your flowers are fully dry, this shouldn't happen. Try drying your flowers for longer and have another go. When dried correctly, the flowers should feel as delicate as tissue paper.

HAS YOUR MOULD LOST ITS SHINE?

- It's time for a new one! Moulds do not last forever and over time they will turn matt and will have to be replaced.

- If your resin piece isn't coming out of the mould shiny and the mould is new, this will most likely be because you have bought a matt mould rather than a shiny one. To be able to create a shiny resin piece you need to use a shiny mould, so do check the inside of the mould before you buy.

ABOUT THE AUTHOR

Mia Winston-Hart is one of the leading jewellers in the resin realm. She is a passionate educator of fellow creatives and an obsessive experimenter. She lives and works in Hampshire, finding inspiration in her surroundings.

A graduate of University of the Arts in London, where she specialized in stitched textiles, Mia discovered jewellery making and the world of resin by chance. She spends her days in her studio, creating small batches of unique and exclusive jewellery, as well as providing education, supplies and much more to the creative community. Originally working with resin to create some botanical hair clips, she now designs moulds from her own drawings to create complex one-of-a-kind jewellery pieces!

In 2020 Mia joined the educators team at Domestika and launched her Resin Jewellery Design online course for beginners, where she shared her processes and working methods for the very first time. Mia believes that resin can be manipulated and used in unlimited ways and she is extremely passionate about pushing the boundaries, experimenting with this exciting medium and encouraging others to do the same.

www.miawinstonhart.com

ACKNOWLEDGMENTS

To Kyle, for always encouraging me to strive to achieve more and to take every opportunity for all it's worth.

To my close friends and family, for supporting me in this crazy and exciting journey over the past few years – you know who you are!

Finally, thank you to my late grandmother, Sonia, for being there at the start, taking me to important interviews and always supporting me, even in her absence.

SUPPLIERS

There are many companies and small businesses that supply materials for working with resin. For the projects in this book I have mainly used supplies from Resin8, including almost all the moulds, with just one or two exceptions as noted in the suppliers details below.

If you are unable to access the exact supplies that I have used, you can, of course, substitute for something similar.

www.miawinstonhart.com (Sixties font mould)

www.resin8.co.uk

www.etsy.com/uk/shop/TawnySupplies (Heart-shaped shaker clip mould)

INDEX

bubbles 27, 28-9, 117

candles 13
coasters 13, 56-9, 60-3
colour 18-19
comb, mermaid 80-3
curing 12, 13, 31, 115, 116

deep pour resin 13, 20, 26, 106-9
drying time 13, 30, 31, 116

earrings 38-41, 50-5, 110-15
epoxy resin 12-13
equipment 8, 17, 22
exothermic reaction 8, 12, 26

flowers 20
    drying 32-3, 117
    engraved fan earrings 50-5
    forget-me-not necklace 46-9
    golden floral key ring 84-7
    keepsake photo key ring 88-91
    layering 20, 30
    pearl-drop earrings 38-41
    positioning 16, 108
    posy paperweight 106-9
foils 20, 56-9, 64-7, 102

glitter 21, 56, 64, 74, 92-5, 96
gloves, safety 8
gold acrylic paint 53

hair clips 92-5, 96-101
hardener 12
heatproof resin 13, 56-63, 74
holes, making 14, 22

inks, alcohol-based 19, 60
inserts 16, 20-1, 30, 32, 42, 88, 96

jewellery
    earrings 38-41, 50-5, 110-15
    findings 23
    flowers 20
    moulds 14
    necklace 46-9
    pendant 42-5
    resin 13
    tools/equipment 22-3
jump rings 22, 23

key rings 84-7, 88-91

layers, working in 26, 30, 38
leaves 32, 42-5, 102-5

mica powder 18
moulds 14-16
    cleaning 16, 17, 116
    custom made 34-5
    de-moulding 31, 116
    problems 116, 117

necklace, forget-me-not 46-9

paperweight, posy 106-9
pendant, into the forest 42-5
petri-dish effect 19
phone case, maple leaf 102-5
pigments 18
polyester resin 12
preparation 8, 17
problem solving 116-17
protective equipment 8

resin
    bubbles 27, 28-9, 117
    colouring 18-19
    measuring 27, 116
    mixing 26-7, 29, 116
    mixing ratio 12, 17, 26
    pouring 28, 29
    safety 8
    setting problems 116-17
    temperature 29, 116, 117
    types 12-13
Resin8 8, 12

safety 8, 13, 16, 17, 19
sanding
    after de-moulding 31, 114
    equipment 17
    safety 8
shaker moulds 14, 96-101
shallow pour resin 12, 20, 26
suppliers 118

table, galaxy side 74-9
tassels 23, 50
techniques 26-35
tools 17, 22
tray
    make up, animal print 64-7
    serving, ocean waves 68-73
troubleshooting 116-17

UV resin 13, 14

work surface, protecting 8, 17

A DAVID AND CHARLES BOOK
© David and Charles, Ltd 2022

David and Charles is an imprint of David and Charles, Ltd
Suite A, Tourism House, Pynes Hill, Exeter, EX2 5WS

Text and Designs © Mia Winston-Hart 2022
Layout and Photography © David and Charles, Ltd 2022

First published in the UK and USA in 2022

ISBN-13: 9781446309094 paperback
ISBN-13: 9781446381441 EPUB
ISBN-13: 9781446381434 PDF

This book has been printed on paper from approved suppliers
and made from pulp from sustainable sources.

Printed in Turkey by Omur for:
David and Charles, Ltd
Suite A, Tourism House, Pynes Hill, Exeter, EX2 5WS

10 9 8 7 6 5 4 3 2

Publishing Director: Ame Verso
Senior Commissioning Editor: Sarah Callard
Managing Editor: Jeni Chown
Editor: Jessica Cropper
Project Editor: Cheryl Brown
Head of Design: Anna Wade
Designer: Sam Staddon
Pre-press Designer: Ali Stark
Photography: Jason Jenkins and Richard Jackson, Forever
Creative Photography
Production Manager: Beverley Richardson

David and Charles publishes high-quality books on a
wide range of subjects. For more information visit
www.davidandcharles.com.

Share your makes with us on social media using #dandcbooks
and follow us on Facebook and Instagram by searching
for @dandcbooks

Layout of the digital edition of this book may vary depending on
reader hardware and display settings.